GOD
IS THE
LIGHT

COLLETTE NLEMCHI

WESTBOW
PRESS*
A DIVISION OF THOMAS NELSON
& ZONDERVAN

WestBow Press books may be ordered through booksellers or by contacting:

WestBow Press
A Division of Thomas Nelson & Zondervan
1663 Liberty Drive
Bloomington, IN 47403
www.westbowpress.com
844-714-3454

Scripture taken from the King James Version of the Bible.

ISBN: 978-1-6642-0393-8 (sc)
ISBN: 978-1-6642-0394-5 (e)

Print information available on the last page.

WestBow Press rev. date: 09/14/2020

CONTENTS

How Wonderful Art Thou 1

Human Beings are So Tiny 2

Days of Abundance 3

The Arm of Flesh 4

Glorious Perfection 5

Glorify Thy God For Success or Failure 6

Put Your Trust in Jesus 7

Oh! Lord Fix My Problems. Plug Yourself in This 8

Thou Art the Light 9

Favor in All I Do 10

Scriptures With Favor of God 11

Heavenly Dialect/Speaking in Tongue 12

No Evil Formed Against Thee Shall Prosper 14

Lifted Up From the Gates of Death 15

Supernatural Faith 16

Thy Ways Oh! Lord is Different 17

Under Your Umbrella 19

God's Declaration 20

The Flowers of Heaven 22

Seek Ye Heavenly Treasures. Matthew 6:19-21 23

Am All That 24

God the King of Kings 25

In Submission 26

Destiny Never Fail 27

Christ the Light 28

I Have No Other Choice 29

Journey of Life 30

Special Blessings 31

The Naked City 32

Thy Will Be Done 33

Author of Redemption 34

Praising God 35

Praise is My Name 36

Sovereignty God 37

Scriptures to Support His Sovereignty 38

Back to Senders 39

Receive Your Blessings 41

Prophecies of Jesus Christ Fulfilled 42

Gates of Righteousness 43

Take Refuge in God 44

Praying For Protection 45

God Attacks Injustice 46

All are Deformed 47

HOW WONDERFUL ART THOU

Thou who answers prayers.
Thou has the whole World in thy Hands.
Thou who appeared to thy chosen Ones.
Thou art Powerful.
And thou art Wonderful.

Your Ways Are Beyond Human Understanding.
Mankind is Ignorant.
However, you let them get away with some Knowledge.
It is you that giveth Knowledge and Wisdom.
It is you that knoweth everything.
It is only you we should adore.

The greatest one who is Compassionate.
I salute you and bow down for you.
You made the Heavens and the Earth.
Thou shall be glorified.
Power of all Powers I salute.

Collette Nlemchi 11/26/19

HUMAN BEINGS ARE SO TINY

When I think about your Wonders,
Humans are smaller than Ants.
This is because all are Imperfect.
Despite all the Wealth and Possessions,
All are Deformed and walket with Clutches unaware.

All are deformed in thy Sight.
We thank you for the Little Chance,
To play at the Field of Dreams.
We are Obedient To thy Command .
On Our Knees We Bow Down.

Thou are really in Control of the Universe.
Under Your Umbrella, we stand.
As you protect us from Dangers.
You know we have tried.
Forgive us our Sins.
As we enter into thy Kingdom.

Collette Nlemchi 11/30/19

DAYS OF ABUNDANCE

Oh! Heaven, I have come again.
Wondering about the Mysteries.
Grateful for the little I have.
And looking forward for the days of Abundance.

I thank you for the days of abundance .
As the days of abundance cometh fast.
I shall humble myself.
Knowing that one who giveth should be honored.

I shall remember the needy on my pathway.
And thou shall direct me as thou giveth.
That which I giveth to the needy.
Shall be honored in your Kingdom.
And I will rejoice and sing with the Angels.

Collette Nlemchi 11/19

THE ARM OF FLESH

The arm of flesh faileth thee.
Depend not on mankind.
Cast your trust in God.
He guideth thy footsteps.
Then pushes Righteous people on your pathway.

Life is not that Roses.
Because he did not promise us smooth journey through life.
Hang in there and do not fuss.
Be faithful and hold strong the word of God.
The word of God is the most precious commodity on Earth.
Receive it as it comes.
And your life will change.

Collette Nlemchi. 2/22/19

GLORIOUS PERFECTION

Oh! Perfection, thou art Holy.
And thou art powerful indeed.
Thou art mysterious and Wonderful.
The mysteries of your Creation.
Makes me to wonder.

Thou maket the Day and Night.
Thou maket the Heavenly bodies.
The Sun, Moon and Stars,
They are bowing down for you.
Talk about the Rivers and the Oceans,
They are singing and clapping their Hands.

Science came trying to prove am all that.
Science cannot create Humans.
But only Robots they can boast of.
Thou art indeed everything.
Thou art Endless.
No beginning and no End.

Man come and go.
And thou livet forever.
I will serve thee all the days of my life.
And thou shall fulfill my Destiny.

Collette Nlemchi 2/22/19

GLORIFY THY GOD FOR SUCCESS OR FAILURE

In the Journey and the Race of This Life,
Thou shall glorify thy God.
In every Race, Glorify thy God.
No matter the Outcome, Glorify thy God.
For Good and For Bad, Glorify thy God.

All you have to do is to try your best.
And live the rest to Faith.
Thou shall glorify thy God in every case.

Those who Mourn recieveth the Oil Of Gladness instead of Mourning.
And Mantle of Praise instead of Spirit of Faint and failure.
Glorify your God Now And Forever.

Collette Nlemchi. 12/22/19

PUT YOUR TRUST IN JESUS

At the lowest point in your life,
Thou shall put your trust in Jesus.
Thou shall have Jesus at the center of your life.

When struggling with life Abnormalities,
Thou shall recite PS 27:1.
The Lord is my Light and he is the one who saves me. I fear no one.

If thou rely on Jesus,
Thou must be saved in this life.
Blessed Assurance I call him.

Collette Nlemchi.12/22/19

OH! LORD FIX MY PROBLEMS.
PLUG YOURSELF IN THIS

Forget Not To Tell Your Heavenly Father To Fix Your Problems.
My Relationship Problems, thou shall fix it Lord.
Known and Unknown Problems, thou shall fix it Lord.
Financial Problems, thou shall fix it Lord.
Confusion Problems, thou shall fix it Lord.
Lack of Favor. Thou shall give me Favor In Jesus Name.
Lack of Sight. Thou shall give me Spiritual Sight In Jesus Name.
Acquaintances. Thou shall provide Spiritual Acquaintances In Jesus Name.
Protection. Thou shall protect me and My Family In Jesus Name.
My Family Problems, Ignorance, lack of Knowledge, Thou shall Fix it Lord.
My Health Problems. Thou shall Fix it Lord.
Enemies. Thou shall Shield and Protect me Lord.
Blockages. Thou shall Remove all Blockages on My Path way Lord.

Collette Nlemchi.1/4/2020.

THOU ART THE LIGHT

Heavenly Father, thou art the light that shines in darkness.
Thou created the Spiritual light for us to see the truth.
Without your illumination we walk in darkness.
When thou walket in the light of God thou seekest wisdom .
Then thou understandeth the truth and the light of his Righteousness.

Thou art the savior, who will help and nourish me.
The fire of the spirit burnet in me.
Thou also are the light that shines and destroy curses in my life.
Thou art also the light that exalt my spirit and soul.
Thou art the light who knows my heart desire.
Thou Oh! Lord is the Speaker of Revelation.

The light exposes that which is in darkness.
With your light I see the truth.
Oh! Lord, I pray, give me light to see that which is hidden.
Thou taket my footsteps away from evil and unrighteousness.

Collette Nlemchi. 1/6/2020

FAVOR IN ALL I DO

From now on, favor is my cup of Tea In Jesus Name.
I command favor of God and Man In Jesus Name.
I command Favor every where I go In Jesus Name.
I command favor over my undertakings In Jesus Name.
I command favor from my Enemies In Jesus Name.
I command favor from those who hate me In Jesus Name.
I command favor of God all around me In Jesus Name.
Oh! Ye favor locate me In Jesus Name.
God's favor be my cup of Tea in Jesus Name.

Collette Nlemchi 1-1-2020

SCRIPTURES WITH FAVOR OF GOD

Matthew5:8
Ephesians 1:11
Proverbs 18:22
Psalms 5:22
Psalms 30:5
Psalms 84:11
Psalms 106:4
Ephesians 2: 8-9
Acts 7: 9-10
Proverbs:3.33-35
Matthew 6: 31-33
Proverbs 3.1-4.

HEAVENLY DIALECT/SPEAKING IN TONGUE

Heavenly dialect is speaking in tongue .Speaking in an unknown language that no one understands except by the interpretation of the Holy Spirit. Most people that speak in tongue does not understand what they speak but the Holy spirit intercede and speak on behalf of the person by using appropriate language which is not corrupt to talk to our Heavenly Father. The Spirit Knows more than we do.

Have your prayer points written down, or memorize what you want. You then pray in Spirit about the prayer points. We human cannot pray the way spirits pray, therefore allow the Holy Spirit to intercede for you.

-Collette Nlemchi.

Praying in tongues is initial evidence or sign that Holy Spirit dwellet . Act 2:4says "And they were all filled with the Holy Ghost and began to speak in an unknown Tongue as the spirit gives utterance.

In 1 Corinthians 14:18, Apostle Paul has this to say" I thank my God, I speak in tongue more than you all."

Speaking in Tongues is like a flowing River that never dries up which eventually, nourishes and enriches one's life spiritually

1 Corinthians 14:2. Write it all down. He that speaket in tongue speaket mysteries

Oh! Lord thy Sovereignty is Supreme.

Speaking in tongue is prayer, Praise and self Edification (1 Cor.14:2) (1 Cor. 14:14) (1 Cor.14:15) (1 Cor 14. 16-17)

Praying in Tongue help us to walk in the Light of God. The Spirit pray according to the will of God, and not according to your will.

NO EVIL FORMED AGAINST
THEE SHALL PROSPER

Worry Not Brethren, God Sees Everything hidden under the Sun. Worry not about Deceptions for the God of the Universe will fight your battle for you.

No evil formed against me shall prosper In Jesus Name.

I Cancel and I Cancel, I Cancel all Deception In Jesus Name.

The Lord has broken the Chain of Darkness In Jesus Name.

Christ is the Light that Shinest in Darkness.

Collette Nlemchi.

LIFTED UP FROM THE GATES OF DEATH

Oh! Heaven, thou has lifted me up from the gates of Death.

The expectation of the Enemies will not come to pass.

I am under the shadow of the Almighty God.

All curses, Sicknesses and diseases are been arrested IN JESUS NAME.

Heavenly father, thou will never forget the needy and the hope of the afflicted will never perish. PS 9. V 18.

Woe unto you, workers of iniquities, thou has fallen into the pit which thou has dug.

PS.9V19: Arise Lord, do not let Mortals Triumph. Let the Nations be Judged in your presence V 20. Strike them with your Terror Lord, let them know that they are only MORTALS.

Collette Nlemchi. 1/15/20.

SUPERNATURAL FAITH

As we live in the world of too many tragedies and injustices, thou heareth the desire of the afflicted,and thou rescue them from their afflictions. It is only you who listens and it is only you who delivers. Oh! Lord, give us the unshakable faith, to receive that which we are asking for. Thou Oh! Lord givet Supernatural Faith. Faith that can move mountains. I receive IN JESUS NAME.

Remember what Jesus said Read Mark 11. 22-24. "What things Soever ye desire when you pray, believe that ye receive them, and you shall have them."

Brethren, have a list of all you want from the Lord, and believe with thy whole heart that thou shall have them and it shall come to pass IN JESUS NAME. Oh! Lord, thou has given the Command, I cannot do it on my own. I ask and beg you to give me the Supernatural faith, and I claim it and so shall it be IN JESUS NAME .AMEN.

Collette Nlemchi

THY WAYS OH! LORD IS DIFFERENT

We have a powerful and Compassionate God. He forgives us our sins and he is the only one who Judges us. Remember, God is a forgiven God, based on the Gravity of your Sin. There are different Categories of Sins and some Sins are Bigger than others, while some Sins are not even considered to be sin by the Lord.

Be careful how you deal with your fellow human being, because when our God is Hurt because of our experiences, those sins goes straight to the Court of Heaven. Because the KING OF KINGS IS HURT because of these activities, the GATES OF HEAVEN WILL NOT OPEN FOR THE WICKED PEOPLE. It really hurt the Lord. And he said: GO THY WAY, thou shall not dwell in my Kingdom.

Oppression of your fellow Human Being is bad. The less fortunate, The Meek, The Rejected, The Abused, The Lowly,, The Ridiculed, Unnecessary wickedness to your fellow human being. Our Lord is Compassionate, he will give you a lot of opportunities to repent and he will forgive. It is totally up to him to execute his Judgement. Some People are Horrible. Remember Matthew 25:31-46. "Whatever you do to the least of my brothers, so you do unto me."

Matthew 25:31-46 . 31 "When the Son of Man comes in his glory, and all the angels with him, he will sit on his glorious throne. 32. All the nations will be gathered before him,and he will separate the people one from another as a shepherd separates the sheep on his right and the goats on his left. READ ALL AND V40 SAYS. "And the King will say, 'I tell you the truth, when you did it to one of the least of these my brethren, ye have done it unto me."

PRAYERS: OH! Lord, help me not to fall into the Sin that Hurts thee as our Heavenly Father. Always direct my foot steps IN JESUS NAME I PRAY . AMEN.

Collette Nlemchi

UNDER YOUR UMBRELLA

Under your umbrella we Stand.

No evil plan shall prevail. (Isaiah 54:17)

The Wicked and Evil Doers shall be punished and Chastised by the Lord.

The God of Heaven and Earth Sees Everything hidden under the Sun.

The God of Heaven and Earth shall protect HIS Chosen Ones. The evil workers working against their Destiny will be CHASTISED AND DESTROYED.

Don't let go your God, be steadfast and serve your God and thou shall see the reward of Righteousness,and it is Doom, Catastrophe and Calamity for the Wicked and Evil Doers.

Put on your oil of gladness for the Lord has rescued you from the hands of your Enemies.

Collette Nlemchi. 1-20-20

GOD'S DECLARATION

I declare that thou art the King of Kings.

I declare that thou Oh! Lord created the whole Universe.

I declare that no Power is Bigger than you.

I declare that all true worshippers of Zion shall not be disappointed.

I declare that me and my family are under your umbrella and no evil shall befall us IN JESUS NAME.

I declare that thou art bigger than Witches, Wizards, Occult, Sorcerers, Native Doctors, Ogboni, and all other hidden and Evil Cults of this World. And thou shall neutralize their powers in my life IN JESUS NAME.

I declare that the destiny you gave me shall not be delayed by Satanic Forces IN JESUS NAME.

I declare that Satanic Delay must stop. IN JESUS NAME.

I declare that me and my Family are taken refuge under your Umbrella IN JESUS NAME.

I declare that God our Heavenly Father, Sitteth at his Holy Throne observing Humanity and their Activities.

I declare that thou Oh! God receives the Righteous and the Wicked is Hail Stones.

I declare that thou Oh! Lord is still on the throne.

I declare that thou art the Omnipotent God.

I declare that thou Oh! Lord shall nourish and fertilize my Talents IN JESUS NAME

Thou shall avoid violence at all cost. Take the matter, problem, or your worriness to the throne of Perfection and thou shall receive an answer. Case Closed.

I declare that I shall meet people that matters, people that will help to advance God's Kingdom on Earth IN JESUS NAME.

I declare that I am one of the chosen ones to advance the Kingdom of God on Earth.

I declare that the KING OF KINGS will protect every movement I take in this world.

The World is full of ignorant and deceptive people, I pray to God to protect me and my family from these Ugly Creatures IN JESUS NAME AMEN.

Collette Nlemchi. 1-20-20

THE FLOWERS OF HEAVEN

Thou Singet Alleluyah to the King.
Thou blossoms with joy .
Thou art happy and fulfilled.
As thou doet the work assigned.

Beautiful Colors you have.
You mysteriously change your Colors.
Thou art something special and glorious.
Your kind does not exist on Earth.
Only spiritual eyes can see thee.
Everlasting happiness you possess.
Flowers of Heaven, I beg you to give me,
A tiny piece to my Possession,
And I shall be made whole and happy.

Collette Nlemchi.2/1/20

SEEK YE HEAVENLY TREASURES.
MATTHEW 6:19-21

Thou shall seek Treasures in Heaven.
Seek not for yourself treasures on Earth.
Where moth, and rust doth corrupt,
And where thieves break through and steal.
V.20. But lay up for yourselves treasures in Heaven,
Where neither moth nor rust doth corrupt.
And where thieves do not break in to steal. Matt:6:19-21

There is a reason for everything .
Cry not and weep not,
He who giveth, taketh away,
You own nothing in this world.
Your possessions are all temporal.
When the time comes, you leave behind all Treasures.
Thou shall seek first the Kingdom of God.
That is where there is the greatest Treasure.
Heavenly Treasures are the best .
There you have Everlasting Happiness.

Collette Nlemchi.

AM ALL THAT

What are things that makes you to say,
I am all that,I am a Christian, I am Rich, I am Bhuda,
I am a Moslem, I am short, I am Tall, I am Black, I am Caucasian,
I have this, I have that, I am Mexican .All these are Vanity .
Remember thou comet to this world alone.
And thou shall die alone.
None can save you at the Court of Heaven.
Thou shall answer for thyself .
Exalteth not thyself with these gifts of God.
The kingdom of God does not have any room for pride.
There is no special or particular Religion in God's Kingdom.
There is no identification in his Kingdom
Mankind glows in the morning
And in a twinkle of an eye,mankind fades and mankind is gone.
Listen! Listen! Listen!. There is absolutely no Religion in his Kingdom.
In his Kingdom, only the Righteous are Chosen.
Irrespective of your Religious practice on Earth.
It does not matter the Color of your Skin, Your Race, Your Height or what
have you.
PRAYERS.OH! LORD forgive us our sins .
And help us to live a Righteous life IN JESUS NAME.

Collette Nlemchi. 9/8/19

GOD THE KING OF KINGS

Heavenly Father, thou art the Head.
The whole Universe under your Shadow.
Thou created this World.
Everything at the palms of your hand.
Thou knowest the activities of every Creature.
And thou knowest it all.
Based on all these, I am under your Shadow.

Thou slaughted famous Kings.
Thou art Everlasting.
And endless is thy name.
Thou cannot be described.
Because thou are changing.
Thou exist at all time.
None can challenge you.

Thou thinkest not like human beings.
Thy ways are different .
Because of all these wonderful attributes of yours,
Thou are my GOD and am under your Umbrella.
Everlasting Daddy, blessed are the true worshippers.
Their foot steps, thou shall direct.

Collette Nlemchi

IN SUBMISSION

Be in Submission to thy Creator.
Believe in him and he will lead you through the storms.
Master of the Universe, thou shall bring those spiritual people on my pathway.
They shall help to fulfil my dreams and shape my Destiny.

My God, thou art a projector of all human imagination.
Thou choses without regard for merit.
Thou art a wonderful God .
And thou giveth us power to play at the field of dreams.

I am in submission to you because .
Thou did set the Boundaries of the Earth. Ps.74.V 17
You made Summer, Winter, Spring, and Autumn.
None participated in thy Creation.
Day and Night are at thy Command.
The whole World and everything at thy Command.
Thou art Wonderful and Thou art Powerful.

Collette Nlemchi

DESTINY NEVER FAIL

OH! Ye my Destiny,
Thou will never fail me .
When I was living in the Spirit World,
Thou made a promise.
And that which you trusted upon me,
Must come to pass.

I shall live to see the manifestation of my Destiny.
Thou Oh! Lord who designate my Destiny,
And thou shall make it to Blossom.
Thank You And Many Thanks For Protecting My Destiny.

Collette Nlemchi. 2/22/20

CHRIST THE LIGHT

Christ is the light that shines in darkness.
Jesus my Savior, thou shall help and nourish me.
Christ is my Savior, and my Helper.
Fire of the Holy Spirit burnet in my life.

Jesus the light of the world.
Jesus the light that shines and destroy curses.
He is the light that exalt my soul.
He is the light that knows my hearth desires.
He is the Speaker of Revelation.

Collette Nlemchi. 12/22/19

I HAVE NO OTHER CHOICE

Come Rain come Sun, I will abide in you.
For the Rivers and the Oceans, I will abide in you.
For the Mountains and trees, I will abide in you.
For the Trees and Vegetations, I will abide in you.
For the Flowers that Sings, I will abide in you.
And we should all bow down for the Supreme Deity.

Collette Nlemchi

JOURNEY OF LIFE

As we move through the Journey of life.
We come across storms, obstacles on the way.
We pass through the Seas, Rivers, and the Oceans.
The Mysteries that surround us makes me to Wonder.
I ask "Is there any of you that can create a single strand of Hair?
The answer is No.
Even my Ancestors cannot solve this puzzle.
I come to conclusion that, there is something beyond all of us.
That mystery is the Creator of the Universe.

Collette Nlemchi

SPECIAL BLESSINGS

Worry not, just count your Blessings.
Be grateful for whatever gift you have.
Be it Big, or Small, be Thankful.
You should know that the God of the Heavens and Earth,
did trust upon us, Special Blessings.
Be grateful for your Talents, Blessing and Accomplishments.

Collette Nlemchi. 2/10/20

THE NAKED CITY

The City I used to know, very far and naked.
At the midst of the desert there she lies.
Tourists come around as they hear her cries.
The birds cry and thirst for waters.
Here comes the strangers from the plane as they landed.
My goodness, I looked up and down.
And could hear the River Sings.
The kind of Songs I used to know.
And these Angelic Songs can bear me witness.
Then I see some Wicked Spirits,
Whose minds are eaten up by worms
Look at me in the Rain and Water
Watering the storm as it pours
OH! My goodness, Heavenly Snow
Look at the Stars as it begins to shine.
My Journey is not in Vain.

Collette Nlemchi . 11-26-06

THY WILL BE DONE

Father, BaBa, I humbly live the World as thou has Created It.
Thou who designet Creation, let thy will be done.
I will try to do my best in this Journey of life.
Thou only knowet what is perfect, and let your will be done.
If my Foot Steps, Decisions, Speeches, Taughts are not in the right order,
Thou Oh! Lord, should guide and redirect my steps.
This is because thou OH! Universe, Knoweth Everything.
I will align my will with thy will, and I ask for thy will to Triumph.
I remember your prayers at the Mount of Olive,
Thou sharest the last meal with the disciples.
Luke 22:42. "Father, if you are willing, take this cup from me, yet not my will,
But yours be done. Luke 22:42.
Thy will should be done, because thou knowet Everything.
I therefore, humble myself before thee, and thou shall take control.
Thou knowet what is best for me.
Thou taket away the Anomalies and Stumbling Blocks.
OH! Universe, thy will be Done. AMEN.

Collette Nlemchi.2/11

AUTHOR OF REDEMPTION

Thou, OH! Lord is the Author of Redemption.
Who designet Creation.
The Universe is at thy Command.
Thy Sovereignty is beyond human understanding.
And thou also is the Speaker of Revelation.
Thou art the highest and Supreme Deity.
Who commanded Creation.
The Saints and Angels Adoreth Thee.
Thou Created both the Big and Small.
All your Creation Adoreth Thee.
And thou Neutralizes and destroy all Evil In Jesus Name.

Collette Nlemchi.

PRAISING GOD

Father, Baba, I adore thee
I will praise your Holy Name
Magnificent Daddy, none like you
Ancient of Days, you are awesome
Miraculous Father, thou are powerful
Omnipotent Daddy, thou art Holy
I will praise thy Holy Name
All the days of my life
I will magnify your name
I will respect a place of worship.
Magnificent Daddy
The Sun, The Moon, and the Heavens Adoreth thee.
Words cannot tell, neither can mouth give enough testimony about your
wonders
Thou art the beginning and thou art the end
Under your umbrella I shall dwell
And thou shall protect every movement and every thing I do.
Holy and magnificent God, who liveth forever.

Collette Nlemchi

PRAISE IS MY NAME

Praise attracts God's presence. (2 Chronicles 7)
As King Solomon dedicated the Temple to God.
He offered sacrifice and praised God.
God answered by sending fire from Heaven.
Then his Glory came down.
Praise attracts the presence of God.
My God goes where he is welcomed.
Praise Assassinate and Crucifies our pride.
Human Nature thinks highly of oneself.
But praise humbles us. Hebrew 13.15.
Regard it as sacrifice of praise.
As we praise, we are being reminded of God's presence in our lives.
Devil Run for its life because he hates praises.
OH! Ye Devil, RUN,RUN,RUN. Am praising my God.
Praise takes me to the Throne of God.

Collette Nlemchi.

SOVEREIGNTY GOD

My God thou art indeed Sovereign.

Thou has the supreme authority over Heaven and Earth.

Thou art the Highest Leader, Highest Deity in all Category and Capacity.

Thou art Powerful, Wonderful, Magnificent and Glorious.

Thou are above all and thou art great indeed.

Thy Sovereignty is above Earthly Kings, Queens and all Other Petty Royalties.

Thou art Wonderful indeed.

Thou art the Highest leader in every Category.

Thou art Powerful.

Thou art in control of all things and a Universal Commander.

Collette Nlemchi

SCRIPTURES TO SUPPORT HIS SOVEREIGNTY

REVELATION: 21:6. "It is done. I am the Alpha and the Omega, the Beginning and the End. To the thirsty I will give Water Without cost from the spring of the water of life. COLOSSIANS 1:16. For in him all things were created: things in Heaven and on Earth, Visible and Invisible, whether thrones or powers or rulers or authorities; all things have been created through him and for him. ROMANS :11:33. Oh! The depth of the riches of the wisdom and knowledge God! How unsearchable his judgements and his paths beyond tracing out! JEREMIAH 32:17. Ah, Sovereign LORD, you have made the heavens and the earth by your great power and outstretched arm. Nothing is too hard for you. PSALM 103:19. The Lord has established his throne in heaven, and his kingdom rules over all.

BACK TO SENDERS

I Command the Holy Spirit to wedge War against my foes IN JESUS NAME.

I Command the Warrior Spirit to attack my attackers IN JESUS NAME.

Oh! Ye the Powerful Spirit, Go right now and Neutralize any evil plans against me IN JESUS NAME.

Holy Spirit, What are you waiting for? Send Hail Stones to Hammer My Enemies who does not want me to succeed IN JESUS NAME.

Holy Spirit, you are the only one that knows about this evil hanging on the Air, I command you to destroy it and right now, send the Arrows back to Senders IN JESUS NAME.

Holy Spirit, me and my Family are under your protection, provide us with your maximum protection IN JESUS NAME.

Holy Spirit, I Command that you stop this Financial Curse, Struggling Life, Delayed and unattainable goals IN JESUS NAME.

Holy Spirit, I receive the good opportunity, and thou shall help me to make it IN JESUS NAME.

Holy Spirit, send on my pathway, people that matters, people that will help me to advance your Kingdom IN JESUS NAME.

Madness and Insanity, Go back to your Senders IN JESUS NAME

Curses back to your Senders IN JESUS NAME.

Witchcraft, Spells, Bad Luck, Confusion, Back to your Senders IN JESUS NAME.

Collette Nlemchi. 12/25/19

RECEIVE YOUR BLESSINGS

I receive long Life, good Health and Prosperity with my Family IN JESUS NAME.

I destroy any Curses of the Womb within my family, IN JESUS NAME.

I receive power to destroy Satan, Serpent, and Scorpions IN JESUS NAME.

I receive Angels of Prosperity dispatched on my path way IN JESUS NAME.

I receive good and smooth Speech IN JESUS NAME.

From now on, Favor is my name. I receive the favor of God and Man IN JESUS NAME.

I Command Favor everywhere I go IN JESUS NAME.

I Command Favor all around me IN JESUS NAME.

OH! Ye Favor Locate Me IN JESUS NAME.

God's Favor be my Cup of Tea IN JESUS NAME.

Collette Nlemchi. 12/25/19

PROPHECIES OF JESUS CHRIST FULFILLED

Many years, decades and Centuries ago, Prophecies upon Prophecies about the Savior was spoken by the Prophets and later on fulfilled. Let us look at some of the Prophecies.

ISAIAH 7: 14. "Therefore the Lord himself will give you a sign: The Virgin will conceive and give birth to a Son, and will call him Emmanuel. FULLFILLMENT......LUKE 1:35

MICAH 5:2. "But you, Bethlehem Ephratah, though thou be little among the thousands of Judah, yet out of thee shall he come forth unto me that is to be ruler in Isreal; whose goings forth have been from of old, from everlasting. FULFILMENT 2:2-6

NUMBERS 24:17: "I see him, but not now; I behold him, but not near. A star will come out of Jacob; a scepter will rise out of Isreal."

ISAIAH 11:1. We know He is from the line of Jesse, the father of King David .;"A shoot will come up from the stump of Jesse; from the roots a branch will bear fruit. The spirit of the Lord will rest on him."

GATES OF RIGHTEOUSNESS

OH! Gates of Righteousness, Open up for me.
I will come into thee.
And I will praise my God.
Thou heareth me.
Thou art my Salvation.
Thou Oh! Lord has shown me Light.
Thou Oh! Lord is my Savior and I will praise and honor thee.
Thy mercy Endureth Forever.
The lord watches over the way of the Righteous.
The ways of the Wicked leads to Destruction. Ps 1.V6

Collette Nlemchi 1/12/20.

TAKE REFUGE IN GOD

Heavenly Father, thou who Created the Universe, I shall take Refuge in thee.
Thou who sitteth at the Highest Throne, I shall take refuge in thee.
Thou who Killeth Death, I shall take Refuge in You.
Thou who destroyeth all kinds of Evil, I will take Refuge in You.
Thou who swallowed every Sorrow, I will take Refuge in You.
Thou who protect your chosen ones, I will take Refuge in You.
Thou who is Everlasting, I shall take Refuge in You.

Collette Nlemchi. 1-12-20.

PRAYING FOR PROTECTION

Thou Oh! Lord, shall hear me in your Righteousness because of my Enemies.

Thou Oh! Lord maket straight my ways.

Thou declared my Enemies guilty and maket their intrigues be their downfall.

Oh! Lord, as I taket Refuge in you, I shall be protected from Satan and evil plans of the Enemy.

Thou Oh! Lord shall bless me and surround me with thy favor and shield.

Heavenly Father, thou has given me Protection from all the hostile forces around me. IN JESUS NAME.

Collette Nlemchi. 1/12/20

GOD ATTACKS INJUSTICE

Hevenly Father, thou art the Owner and Creator of this World.

Whoever that is pregnant with mischief, Conceiveth or gives birth to Catastrophy. Ps7:14.

Whoever, that digs a hole, falls into it.Ps7:15.

The trouble they cause recoils on them, their violence comes down on their heads. Ps 7:16.

I will give thanks to the Lord because of his righteousness, I will sing the praises to the Lord most High.

Thou Evil, thou has fallen into the pit you dig for others.

Thou hater, you are hated.

Thou deceiver, thou art deceived.

Thou gossiper you are the Victim.

Be careful who you mess with.

Collette Nlemchi 1-12-20

ALL ARE DEFORMED

Oh! Heavenly Father, I adore and honor thee.
Thou who Created Heaven and Earth.
It is only you Lord, that is Perfect.
Ignorant and Stupidity has blindfolded Humanity.
They knowet not the facts of life.
Envy not the prosperity of the Wicked .Ps 73:3
Today he is and Tomorrow, he is no more.
Where thou goeth, no one can tell.
It is always good to be good and compassionate to the needy.
Thou, then shall enter into the Kingdom of Perfection.
Laugh not at one's deformity because, thou also is deformed.
As long as thou liveth, thou shall see deformity.
Word of advice, be kind to the deformed, so that your Father in Heaven
will let you in.
Thou art very Rich and thou laugh at the poor.
When Sickness comes, thou art Helpless, Brainless, and totally deformed.
Boast not, because of thy Wealth, because life is full of Drama.
His ways are different from our ways.
Humans are like Roses,
Roses Blossom in the morning and fades at Night.
Boast not with that, which fades.
Use your gift to offer help to the less fortunate, and thou shall be glorified
by the Lord.
PRAYERS: Oh! Lord, help me to use the little gift I have to Enlighten
Humanity.IN JESUS NAME.

Collette Nlemchi. 3/7/20

Printed in the United States
By Bookmasters